PHOENIX **POETS**

MARK HALLIDAY

J A B

THE UNIVERSITY OF CHICAGO PRESS
Chicago and London

MARK HALLIDAY teaches in the creative writing program at
Ohio University. He is the author of three books of poems,
Little Star, Tasker Street, and *Selfwolf,* the last published by the
University of Chicago Press. His study of Wallace Stevens,
Stevens and the Interpersonal, was published in 1991. In 2001,
he received the Rome Prize in Literature from the American
Academy of Arts and Letters.

The University of Chicago Press, Chicago 60637
The University of Chicago Press, Ltd., London
© 2002 by The University of Chicago
All rights reserved. Published 2002
Printed in the United States of America

11 10 09 08 07 06 05 04 03 02   1 2 3 4 5

ISBN: 0-226-31385-9 (cloth)
ISBN: 0-226-31386-7 (paper)

Library of Congress Cataloging-in-Publication Data

Halliday, Mark, 1949–
    Jab / Mark Halliday.
       p. cm. — (Phoenix poets)
    ISBN 0-226-31385-9 (cloth : alk. paper) —
    ISBN 0-226-31386-7 (pbk. : alk. paper)
    I. Title. II. Series.

    PS3558.A386 J33 2002
    811′.54—dc21

                                        2002020402

♾ The paper used in this publication meets the minimum
requirements of the American National Standard for
Information Sciences—Permanence of Paper for Printed
Library Materials, ANSI Z39.48-1992.

To feel trivial and idiotic and to live with this feeling is to be a hero in a way that no god can be.

— STEVIE SMITH

Flux is victorious but cannot accept the award.

— MICHAEL THEUNE

I have heard that a genuine artist
isn't recognized till she is dead.
But I thought you might like the pig on a trike
with a pudding on top of its head.

— HELENA NELSON

Contents

Acknowledgments

Grateful acknowledgment is made to the editors of publications in which these poems, or versions of them, first appeared:

Algonquin (Ohio University–Zanesville): "Campaign Promise"
Black Warrior Review: "Nights at Ruby's," "Scale"
Colorado Review: "The Opaque"
CrossConnect: "Campaign Promise" (as "And If I Am Elected")
Harvard Review: "Dennis Pravy Speaks"
Michigan Quarterly Review: "The Beloved"
New Orleans Review: "Sourdough"
The Phoenix Literary Section (Boston): "Separated Father"
Poetry Review (London): "Contents," "Cotton Club Classics," "Seven Baskets,"
        "Trumpet Player, 1963"
Slate Magazine (www.slate.com): "Divorced Fathers and Pizza Crusts," "The
        Fedge," "Parkersburg," copyright 1998, 1997, and 1999. Reprinted
        with permission.
Sycamore Review: "Summer 1935"

"Parkersburg" appeared in *Poets of the New Century,* edited by Roger
        Weingarten and Richard Higgerson (Boston: David R. Godine
        Press, 2001). Reprinted by permission of David R. Godine, publisher.
"Schnetzer Day," "Sourdough," and "Why Must We Write?" appeared in *The
        Breath of Parted Lips: Voices from the Robert Frost Place* (Fort Lee, N.J.:
        CavanKerry Press, 2001).

Time in a Brown House

Sam paused on the stairs. He had forgotten a thing.
In Leland's room a copy of Thomas Merton lay on the floor.
The air was full of gnats of possibility. What was the story?
Sam looked at the clock twice. The day was dropping
softly away while Sam's sneakers made the wood stairs creak.
The wood was sure it was wood. Alice got home from the store.
The bags had to be unloaded as the day went and went.
Then the sundown kitchen grew quiet.
Sam crossed his legs one way, then the other way. He had chosen
purple corduroys. They were pants of the day; one possibility.
On the tilted table sat the damaged typewriter.
What about Thomas Merton? Did he know the central story?
Someone was quietly reading by the fireplace but not Sam.
Next day there was badminton with the troubled carpenter
and the story of an awful egg salad, causing laughter;
but Sam had forgotten some thing. Then Alice brought in
the brownies and minor pleasure colored the house

and there went the evening. J.J. came downstairs
all gleamy from her bath. She had three reasons to get downtown fast.
Sam picked up a novel by Sukenick. The clue must be nearby.
Between Sam and the page swarmed the gnats of possibility.
Leland stowed his bicycle in the basement and came upstairs
with a point about capitalism. Look at the time said someone.
Where was J.J. now? Where was the story? Under the red chair
lay the newspaper whose relevance was all mystery or

not mystery enough. Then Alice went out to see a movie.
Some man meets some woman with big eyes on a jet
and changes his whole life for her, disastrously but thrillingly.
Alice told about it briefly, and went to make tea. Sam paused
on the hard wooden stairs. J.J. was gone. She was gone.
Leland was eating yogurt at midnight. The whole brown house
was floating, gliding very smoothly for some reason
with Sam not clear whether the gliding was a story
and if so was it central and was it his?

The Pink Car

The pink car is in my head.
It rolls calmly and calmly.
Across the carpet in 1957 and in my head.

Why is it pink? The question does not come up.
The pink car is just what it is and glad so.
Pink is its own color, of its own, being that,
calmly along the quiet roads.

(Pink not anything about sex
and not anything about femininity
and not anything about embarrassment or socialism
those meanings are from outside
whereas this pink car is not coming from an idea
it is a way of being its own self.)

The pink car rolls slowly along a pale green lane
till it needs to go fast then it goes very fast
while still quiet. It knows what it is,
it is the pink car!

Along the lanes to be what it is
it goes around hard corners and far across a wide plain
and back again whenever it wants.
Other cars can be all those other colors
the pink car doesn't care they can be loud and big

the pink car doesn't care that is why it can roll
so quietly and go slow until it goes fast for a while.

Other cars might honk their horns to seem big—
the pink car doesn't honk and doesn't worry
it just goes along the pale green lane
and around a sharp corner and down another lane
to stop in a special spot. Why is the spot special?
Because the pink car stopped there!

Stopping quiet but ready to go, to go
and be the pink car which is all it wants.
And when will I, when can
I ever be the man
implied by that sedan?

Thirteenth Round

Darkness pummeled the U-Haul cab.
Eternity whispered "Stifle the gab."

Biology said "You'll be carved on a slab.
Your name will boil down to labels in a lab."

Nothingness poked at me like a crab.
"How many peaches can a dead duck grab?"

A former lover said my writing showed flab.
I thought it over. I cherished the scab.

I cried "This road leads from drab to fab!"
Time grinned "Sure. It's all on the tab."

"But my rhymes," I muttered, "are loved by Queen Mab."
I quoted some Keats. I threw another jab.

Summer 1935

We three spent a lovely afternoon and evening
in Brooklyn Heights, taking a swim at the St. George Hotel
and more or less destroying in the broiler at my parents' apartment
the filet mignon we had extravagantly purchased for dinner
along with a bottle of cheap red wine
that John selected, in view of our depleted funds,
with exquisite care.
It was me and Jane and John

in the flickering light of summer remembered,
we three in the laughter of the narrow kitchen,
there in an actuality of what was
with the noise of dishes and the smell of burned steak
and the sense of giving oneself up to life
in the dark taste of the cheap red wine.
Afterward we went up and sat under the canopy on the roof,
watching the Staten Island ferries whose lights
were like the things we said, sparkling bravely
in the darkness of summer remembered.
It was John and Jane and me.

Fifty years later I tell my son a little of it,
talking about friendship, and he tries to listen,
but he doesn't hear the slam of the broiler door,
Jane's smart giggle on the steps to the roof, or
John's oddly high-pitched laugh constricted by

his next allusion to Shakespeare.
My son remembers that kitchen and that roof
as places of grapefruit juice and balsa-wood airplanes
in his own life. In my life, one day in Brooklyn Heights

it was me and Jane and John
cooking expensive meat and drinking cheap red wine
and creating together one more eventual chance
for me to be naturally lonely
as the only person who ever lived my life—

but the lights out there on the Bridge and on the Chrysler Building
were lit for us.

          . . . I say that, and I feel the Poetic Truth in it.
But I know that to say it is a kind of work—

it's the work of keeping down the other truth,
the one about how a decade is ten minutes,
the one that points to bottles and cow bones in the trash.

At the edge of the great level dark roof we stood,
we three, telling stories about our absent-minded teachers
who forgot damn near everything except what they really loved.

The Man Who Is Not at the Table

Now that my humorous friend is dead
and from the world is deleted
he does not sit at the long table in the dining room,
the long table whose faded green tablecloth can be described
as gentle and modest by someone alive
in a world just waiting for adjectives. He does not sit there

reading a book he hasn't looked at since grad school,
bemused by his own marginal jottings—
"Art as illusion? Or is this ironic?"—seeing
an idiosyncratic merit in phrases that once provided only
promptings for lunch-hour parodies in that courtyard
where the yellowjackets obsessed over our sandwiches . . .
He's not there

at the table in such a way
that someone could notice his dark reflection
in the glass pane that protects a watercolor of beached boats,
his reflection dark-shadow-gray but not black
framed by the oddly bright reflection of the red and white curtains
behind him filtering winter afternoon sunlight
with a quiet complication

that someone usually might skim over
as if there would be plenty of time to go back
and really ponder the bits that seemed elusive
or just not crucial to the main theme
the first time through.

Olivier Bergmann

Olivier Bergmann. Hotel owner, war veteran, reader of Kafka—

I remember the twinkle fierce in your eyes beneath your bristling brows
in the dining room of Hotel Le Clos in 1967. Twinkle
is a word that can't be used seriously in poetry but
what is the good alternative? Gleam won't do.
What is the French word, it seems to be *pétillement*—
that may be fine in French but here I don't feel how to use it—
payteemonh . . . Olivier:

your fierce eyes—your glance was tough on adolescent reverie;
not many people now can remember *le pétillement de vos yeux*
but I can, Olivier Bergmann.

As a seventeen-year-old waiter and porter in your hotel
I was such a bumbly American boy giraffe
and you were so impatient with me but you strove honorably
to contain your impatience so I wouldn't be terrified
and your twinkle, though fierce, somehow saved me from cowering.
Tell us, Mark, what kind of twinkle was it exactly?
It was a twinkle that said:

"It is true we have strange infinity within us;
my own is darkly strange; but we have to live
in the physical world of shops, onions, coal, beef,
we cannot disdain the actual for then the actual would

triumph over us, we must refuse to be humiliated by the actual,
hence we will prepare and serve *le petit déjeuner* to our guests
with maximum efficiency and it will arrive at the rooms *hot*.
This we will do with a graceful kind of brusqueness
because death is in the world, our only world. *Jeune homme,*
we will do this work never forgetting
the absurdity known to Kafka
nor the evil done by sick envious preening cowardly politicians
nor the beauty of not surrendering. Now
go on, go!"
          And I grabbed the breakfast trays
which I had prepared too slowly and lurched off
along the narrow corridors to do my job hoping I might
slightly briefly please Olivier Bergmann.

Impatiently blinking beneath those bristling brows
now in my mind Olivier you seem to say
"No true twinkle gets caught in such easy words, Mark"
or maybe you're saying
"*Donc, voilà, c'est un poème, et bien,* what next?"

Poetry Failure

For example, I wrote a poem in 1976 about being in the Vermont house
after my mother's death; she died the year before;
she loved that house. My father said he kept having moments
of thinking she must have just stepped outside for a minute
to weed the garden or to walk just a little way
along Prospect Street, for a few minutes only and now
almost now she'd be coming back, we'd hear the screen door,
Bev would be back and saying something casual about—

about the cats, Daphne and Chloe, or about Mrs. Yamokofsky next door
or about the pear tree, "or a colored stone she found."
That was the phrase that ended my poem in 1976:
"or a colored stone she found." The phrase rang slightly false
but I wanted it—the "ound" and "one" sounds sounded profound
and in 1976 "stone" was still a word guaranteed poetic.
But did my mother ever pick up colorful stones?
Wasn't that more something I did fifteen years earlier?
In the poem I was trying to turn my ironic mother into
an ideal figure certified sweet like a child.

But what could I make her say? Something very sly and wry?
The poetry would be in her voice, the way of her voice being
hers—voice of my mother—whether the words were about
the cats or Mrs. Yamokofsky or potatoes to peel for mashing.
Not *your* mother. *My* mother. Poetry of her
saying in her Bev way "those potatoes" or "Mrs. Yamokofsky"

or "Daphne's gone down by the Black River
but if we feed Chloe I'm sure she'll be back."
And my father and Kimbo and me just going "Yeah" or "In a minute"
because this was all just life.

The Sunny Ridge

In my dream my mother was alive, talking with her friend
Madame de Piolenc, in beach chairs on a sandy ridge
just outside a screened enclosure of shade. They sat
in mild sunshine talking intently; and I knew they were
there, though I was with others down the hill
in some clacking room of noise like a small train station
and the people all wanted to relocate, for further fun,
they were flapping like ducks with sunglasses,
they were caught up in the pleasing social confusion
and they said "Come on here we go" but I said
"I have to get my mother"
                                    so she would not miss
the picnic or whatever and they all understood
so then I walked fast among pines up the shady hill
carrying a shishkabob skewer loaded with tomatoes and onions
and I entered the screened enclosure and blinked,
then through the shady screen I saw my mother,
saw her brown hair so lightly streaked with strands of white
over the back of her beach chair where she leaned
a little sideways to listen to Madame de Piolenc,
so then I moved carefully through the door trying
not to disturb other people who sat on the sunny ridge,
anxious not to poke them with my loaded skewer;
and my blue shirt snagged on a hook but only
for a second and then
                                    I did reach my mother,

she and Madame de Piolenc smiled because I seemed anxious
and because their conversation had been so wry and amusing
and I did tell my mother about the picnic
and how much everyone hoped she'd rejoin the group.

Head Wound

On the day that my life span matched my mother's life span,
on the day when I had come to live as long as my mother lived—
she died in 1975, of cancer, three days after her fifty-second birthday—
on the day when I had lived as many days as she got to live
(though for her there were hundreds and hundreds of days of
miserable pain, which has not at all been my fate)—
on that day
I went to the gym to play basketball with some friends.

The game was fun, intense, chaotic—
trying to steal a rebound from big Patrick
I got my head in a wrong conjunction of time and space
and his big elbow hit me hard—I staggered
and muttered "I'm okay I'm okay" but everyone said "No you're not"
and my hand came scarlet from my head.
They made me sit down, and someone ran for towels and ice.
There was a silence in the universe for perhaps ten seconds
and it seemed to clang with meaning.

To see if I had a concussion one guy asked me questions
like today's date and my age and I told him.
Minutes later, when it was clear the cut on my head was superficial,
everybody spoke knowingly about head wounds
like a staff of doctors who can't be fazed—
"Head wounds, man, yeah, they bleed like a river" . . .
But I remember their eyes in that ten-second silence:

human beings in the presence of something—fate—
their eyes all remarkably sober and focused and interested
watching my eyes as I mopped ineffectually at the bright red stream
crossing my forehead and dripping to darken my blue teeshirt
with strange implication.

Driving to the Emergency Room I had seven thoughts:
1. It's a reminder.
2. It's a warning.
3. Let's not get carried away.
4. No wonder it is necessary and has always been necessary
   to read poems and write them, to read novels and write them,
   because the world is this enormous haunted cavern or enchanted gymnasium
   filled, too filled with symbolic meanings ready at any moment
   to spring forth like goblins and make anything significant.
5. I'm lucky, she wasn't lucky;
   she wasn't lucky, I'm lucky, it doesn't mean
   ANYTHING—
6. But even if it doesn't, I can still say
   her bad luck was bad;
7. And if that's true, doesn't it follow
   that my good luck is good?

Scale

Above Manhattan in the late winter night a jet passes
with its roar negligible at twelve thousand feet
as my father and me we spread mayonnaise

very carefully on our rye bread for late sandwiches
far down here in Manhattan in the tiny filmy kitchen.
He is eighty-six and I am fifty-one.

So carefully we spread our mayonnaise
and upon it we arrange our ham and Swiss.
Father and son in the city night

negligible, focused on sandwiches, bending
toward our ham and Swiss slices, are we
a sad spectacle? Terribly sad?

I don't know why you ask that.
The question is uncivil, it is out of scale,
I challenge you to say what put it in your mind.

Who are you at all?
Are you a jet pilot of eternity?
I think not.

Are you the Mayor of a city where kitchens don't get grime-coated
and old boys don't rely on small small pleasures?
I very much doubt it.

(Are you a serious campaigner for the welfare of pigs?
Please.)
Well then be quiet.

Be quiet and let the poem (unlike life) end on the word "together".
Down far here in Manhattan father and son we
watch a movie in which the characters make

awesome suave mistakes
in the mythic city of being forever thirty
and we eat our homemade sandwiches together.

Summer Planning

My father and I on the sofa talked about summer plans,
would he drive from New York to Ohio?
It seemed doubtful (he was eighty-six)
and he said We'll see what comes to pass.
For a minute we were silent.
He said, That's an interesting idiom, isn't it.
To come to pass. "It came to pass."
There's a feeling of both coming and going
at the same time.
Yeah, I said. I wondered what movie we might see.
He said, It's quite different to say "It happened"—
that sounds like a stop, like a fixed point.
But "It came to pass"—there's almost a feeling of
"It came in order to pass."
Yeah, I said, that's right.
He said, You get a sense of the transience of everything.
Yes, I said.
Cleo the black cat lay snoozing across my father's legs.
My father stroked her gently.
I finished my raspberry iced tea.

Strawberry Milkshake

This is my medium strawberry milkshake.

Well what did you want it to be?
Not this because it's too boojy?
It's too what, too dairy and Oklahoma?
Okay so then what did you want—should we just maybe
let it be you and your thing?
Because I admit, what I've got is going to be—
is mainly going to come down to this balding curly head,
this boy's life, bag of loss chips and wish caps, pastel maps
of a dreambreezed kingdom named Sam Bass
whose riverboats carry me toward each girl
I could not kiss in 1967.
                    Sure,
I could try to imply some universal pattern, relevance to certain persons
you failed to kiss in 1988 but you're still going to feel this is
my own blandished finger-smudged bland dish
of warped middle-class Creedence albums and Red Sox sweatshirt
and Oh-God-that-blonde-across-the-street
and fetishizing my son's toy trains
and my daughter's way of singing "Yet's go fwy a kite"

—you see what I mean, to you
it's all just my own medium strawberry boojy milkshake

so let's give it over! Let's do *you*. Let's hear
only exactly what's missing for you, what is it,
a frozen daiquiri with someone whose spouse is dying?
Is it your father's Buick and everything it means
about power and neglect in America?
Who *did* you kiss in 1988 and how far past the lips did you go?
And what did you find there?
I could care. On some days I could.
Your sibling plays with drugs
whose names I can't even spell. Religion
looms like a greenish flickered fog above the glen
of your fear of what goes wrong with love. Does it?
The drill bites down into the two-by-sixes
emitting a real-world whine
and it's that whine and bite you miss and that daiquiri
and a funky funky funky Brazilian restaurant in NYC
and Brazilian sex, Brazilian money, Brazilian churches,
Cameron Diaz at a party, leather-lads in East Berlin,
profound awareness of Stravinsky and Charlie Parker,
sawed-off self-destructiveness of your former friend in dirty red shoes.
Right? So let's

put all that in and like stencil it very sharp across this evening air.
For you.
And put in your particular hospital sadness
and your night-side of Nashville,
your poxed village in Ukraine,
put in your comedy of computer hacking
and your misgiving as to whether the sparrows' flight encodes
a goddess kin to Moneta; include

your bitter tumescence, your deliquescence . . . Whatever works!
I will just sit right here. I won't mutter at all.
At last you'll have the language
you've been looking for in those blue hours
that live inside minutes, and somebody will be happy.

Contents

Your Table of Contents foretells disappointment.
At a glance we can see how selective it is—you've selected
what doesn't cut deep. The result is a pleasantness—
as if the book were dressed for a party where the snacks are
nifty and expensive.

You include "Charming Young Man Eating Spanish Rice"
and "Charming Midlife Man Sipping Cappuccino"
and these are probably appealing in some way—in the way of
cool comfortable entertainment . . .
But Janet is not here, Janet who said, years back,
"Some promises are not made in words."
And in a hotel lobby there was a child who said
"I don't want to say goodbye because that means you're leaving."
This, with the veins pale blue in the child's right temple,
this is missing.

What you offer nearly vanishes beneath the silent hoofs
of the all-night stampede of what you don't offer.

We flip around in the book and we get itchy.
You give us your ode to red hair,
and an ode to women seen on public transit;
and the ballad of sweet lonely you on the wrong train from Hamburg to
    Wurzburg.
You give us your ode to a Royal typewriter

and "Poem on Poems About Writing"
and your sonnet cycle "Maybe Maybe I'm Lovable"
and your lampoons of poets with Big Deep Masculine Hearts;
plus many jeux d'esprit involving muddy swans and small potatoes.
Also you offer an elegy for a touchdown pass thrown in 1964
at Coleytown Junior High School, along with
elegies for fifteen gentle normal hungers attached to fifteen songs

and these are not worthless, we don't say they're worthless
but our skin itches, our fingers writhe, our jaws clench
in this air of *omission*—

where is the little boy deep in Philadelphia who loved yellow raisins?
Not just his image but everything his existence meant;
and where is the dull blue wall of a construction site
across from St. Luke's Hospital the morning of your aunt's death?
Where, where is some study of your casual blind uncaring
in Providence, Syracuse, and Waltham?
Where is your sense of walking festooned in failure,
a fanning peacock of failure?
We don't find that in the Contents here!

We want to turn the page and read "What I Tried to Articulate
But Forfeited Due to Convention". That's nowhere
in this pleasant book . . . And you don't even include
the weariness of still trying to rock with the Rolling Stones
along a 3 A.M. highway in Ohio thirty years after "Exile on Main Street"—

do you? Oh maybe you do "to some extent". But in the dark byways of thought
you too must hear pounding those *silent hoofs*
and feel, like us, this itchy lack in the hazy humid moonlight.

Cotton Club Classics

Elsewhere a trumpet plays. It is quite possibly
Louis Armstrong in his Cotton Club phase, if that was a phase,
but I don't hear it. I am not
hearing it; and would not be ready rightly to listen
if I were there. Instead je slump ici with this silence
of not having found—of the unplayed music of not having selected . . .
Some people are sure. "I can't stand Richard Rorty"
says the young theorist with strong eyebrows and legs.
Trumpet, elsewhere. At a party in Sausalito
some man in a black shirt says "Fritz Lang and Werner Herzog"
or "The fig needs the hornbill as much as the hornbill needs the fig"
and two women lean closer to him
but I wasn't invited and if I were there I wouldn't have caught
what the man said; I would be dipping my tiny shrimp in cocktail sauce
and pretending to look at someone's article on ambiguity in Jane Austen
nine miles or 2800 miles away from the life-changing contact—

in a restaurant whose name is a winking foreign word
a woman in her early thirties laughs and her teeth flash like a trumpet.
The startling candor of her gaze makes someone think of
the actress Elisabeth Shue and it's a galvanizing thought
but I'm not there to think it because my choices
which overlap so extensively with my slumpy fears have kept me
at another table pinching up bits of potato from the tablecloth;
and like her teeth and laugh and gaze in some way
is a book in the hands of someone in—

is it Chapel Hill? Is it Baltimore? Or it might be Hampstead—
someone reading till 2 A.M.
wearing an old blue shirt and a light cotton sweater,
the book kindling a sudden sense of how one's fate gets made,
a book I passed over in a bookstore last year,
my hand not quite brushing it on the shelf.

Nights at Ruby's

Jane leaned toward us across the table at Ruby's
to make a point about a book. This was 1954
and her point was sharp. Her nose was sharp
in a good way, this was a type of beauty,
this was beauty with edge. Jane's fingers were long
tapping the table in 1954 at Ruby's
to make her excellent unexpected point about a book

and there were no other tables, no other cafes,
no other streets that could matter at all
as we were so smart-funny together
saying "lizard wisdom" and "black umbrellas of fate"
and "the motif motif" and "Ginger breaks free
in Chapter Three." There was no place else.

And so

if you speak of Wendy with two-color hair
leaning across some table at Como's in 2001
to make some arguably cogent point about some derivative book
in 2001, for godsake, I can barely hear you,
you speak from behind so many scrims of gauze
with your little voice so thinned and vagued
by the wrongness of it not coming from Ruby's in 1954—

I want to feel embarrassed for you
as you lean forward claiming some Wendy was so smart
in Dobo's or Como's in 2001,
2001 a year so disastrously unimportant!
You say Wendy's hands hilariously shaped a plot in air
and the five syllables of "hilariously" sound so presumptuous,
so exorbitant, so unweighed, so deeply uninformed,
you actually say that in 2001 Wendy's eyes "sparkled"
as she called some book *Esther Goes Wester on the Retro Metro*—
that's a tinsel kind of sparkle, it wipes off in a blink
but you can't see why. Please don't talk so loud.
You and your zippy friends,

you're drowning the beauty of 1954
and you can't even hear the ship going under
and it's me, what meant me, what I meant to know as me

so I am going to wake up early each morning
and think of sarcastic things to say to keep you small.

Against Realism

She is over there, at the edge, just past
what I can really notice. She wears brown shoes
and she has two jobs probably, like
financial records work for small businesses and, evenings,
behind-the-counter at a convenience store.
Why the need for extra cash? I don't like the dry way she says "cash"—
maybe she has twin daughters age nine, or her husband got laid off,
or both, who knows, she has this dry vibe of dismissal
like "That seemed fun when I was nineteen
but now I know there's only dust and being decent"
anyway her life is pinched and it's not her fault okay
and she deals with it bravely I suppose
although "bravely" makes it sound interesting whereas I just feel
it is so dreary I can't even focus on it
and she herself realizes it's not heroic, it's just being an Adult
and Coping. Frankly I hate the way she uses the word "coping"
and I would prefer never to hear the word again from anybody.
In her voice there's this tone that says "A dreamer is a parasite,"
not that she would ever explicitly say something that intense
because she is thinking about daycare and the dinner.
I know I should admire how she works and plans and keeps up
with the laundry, whatever, and feeds the dog
and visits her sick uncle, whatever,
okay I do, in principle, but between you and me
she is so boring in her, you know, her busy life of hardihood and pathos,
God, when you have to pause and face it

there is nothing more deadly than hardihood-and-pathos,
I mean it really kills the secret thing—
the non-dust thing—the vital electric bloomy comet leopard secret
symphony heart.
If I have to think admiringly one more minute on how
she starts the pot roast at dawn and brushes Jenny's hair
and how to her sex is mainly the problem of unwanted pregnancy
which she counsels younger women about so helpfully
and how she is supportive, she is so supportive
I swear I will pass out and fall down and get a boredom-induced concussion
or else write only fantasy fiction disguised as bitter satire
or else give up and become a decent concerned citizen
and disappear into the brown huge hum-hum of all that human decent pathos,
that brown-shoe humanity always there, over there
on the side at the edge where thank God I'm not looking.

Lunch with Big Steve

Arkady the theorist told me on a hot sidewalk
that my notion of telling the truth is charmingly naïve.
Poems should be aggressively fictive
since fictivity is mandated anyway. I *guess* I dig.
Life *is* that thing going yopso vut blut vut blut kjang
around the edge of what you say it is and through
the very veins of what wasn't exactly said or heard;
amidst some party or some lecture on the treachery of signifiers
you think of your mother's kindness to the Mercier girls
one of them is dead now and in the car going down the driveway she sang
"Runaround Sue" in the world of extreme fear of kisses.
At the same time virtually you think of too-young Joann unkissed
she of the sharp nose she attracts you too much and
yesterday she startled you with an offer of strawberries
which became the idea that she might transform your buzzbuzz life
with juicy forbidden love all this amidst
                                    NOW the next day which is
now when talk is happening with big Steve and Dan and Dan's brother
and your wife all looking for lunch in your life and if
this noise including your own mosquito-like jokes isn't your life
your "true" life then you may have a problem; are you a cloud?
The traffic is metal-shiny the air is warm the bricks are warm the shop is open
your feet are fast you want something! It is not only lunch!
Is truth another name for desire? What do I mean?
Gone like strawberries now dubbadow dubbadow

so the sensible clear story of any lunch or marriage risks our contempt
because we feel
the omission of strawberry fear juice dream depth as well as
the omission of kjang, yopso, shreff, bshunk, gesproomboom, floymoy—
that's two kinds of omission isn't it? Ashbery
he knows this like he knows his own name. At lunch

big Steve wears a bright orange shirt like a barrel of Tang
and reflector sunglasses. He is a bubbling vat
of rhapsodic lunch comedy in the pizza place on Spruce—
when you say "The waiter's not coming" Steve says
"I had that problem once after twelve beers, the lady wept on my chest."
Big Steve orders an Italian hoagie with oil, he may speak lasciviously of
lubrication someone else is talking maybe he did
now the topic is Dan's brother being interviewed on local TV
about a Ticketron scandal he cares a lot
everyone at the table seems to care except you
and if this isn't your life if you feel the TRUE life is elsewhere
you may have a problem, but after all tickets *are* chances to see
the singers who give our lives fictive shape
why doesn't this thought make you take an interest you keep glancing
out the hot window three people are talking at once
the sandwiches are good for what they are but you are afloat
alone on an ocean of talk and possibly now sinking—what?
Big Steve has made five more jokes Dan is explaining "slap-back"
a musical technique employed by Charlie Feathers
and your wife is sharing her home fries—
                                        it's all fine it's all swell
but no grasp no hold no expression of the jangle in its true kjang
and no strawberries of delusory Joann no heart of cloudy heart so
everything not expressed; Arkady wins—to an extent—
dubbadow
dubbadow somebody said a thing big Steve is laughing and winking

everybody drinks Cokes yopso if this is not de troot for you
or if this is not the kind of truth you want to try (and fail) to express
then you may have problems in future
                                        vut blut vut blut
absent lips "Scooter lookin' for his groove" what? You
don't quite catch—kjang, kjang,
frujnuj

Trumpet Player, 1963

And when I get to Surf City I'll be shootin' the curls,
And checkin' out the parties for surfer girls.

When Jan and Dean recorded "Surf City"
there must have been one guy—

I see this trumpet player (was there even a horn section in that song?
Say there was)—

I see this one trumpet player with his tie askew
or maybe he's wearing a loose tropical-foliage shirt
sitting on a metal chair waiting
for the session to reach the big chorus
where Jan and Dean exult
Two girls for every boy
                    and he's thinking
of his hundred nights on his buddy Marvin's hairy stainy sofa
and the way hot dogs and coffee make a mud misery
and the way one girl is far too much and besides
he hasn't had the one in fourteen months, wait,
it's fifteen now.
Surfing—what life actually lets guys ride boards
on waves? Is it all fiction? Is it a joke?
Jan and Dean and their pal Brian act like it's a fine, good joke

whereas this trumpet player thinks it's actually shit,
if anybody asked him, a tidal wave of shit.
Nobody's asking.
The producer jiggles in his headphones. He wants more drums
right after *all you gotta do is just wink your eye!*
This producer is chubby and there is no chance,
my trumpet player thinks, that this chubhead gets
two swingin' honeys at any party ever and besides
on a given night a man only has one cock, or
am I wrong? And besides, you wake up wanting five aspirin
in an air lousy with lies, or half-lies.
And that's with only one girl.

But why am I so pissed here, he thinks,
when all these guys are hot for a hit?
Because I'm deep like Coltrane and they're all shallow,
right? Or because
I'm this smelly sour session man with a bent nose
and they're all hip to this fine fine joke?

The song is cooking, it's nearly in the can,
everybody has that hot-hit look
and my trumpet man has a thought: Sex
is not really it—what they're singing about—
they're singing about being here.
This dumb song is *it:*
this studio, this is the only Surf City,
here. And that's the great joke.

Okay, surf dicks, I am hip. But
there's gonna be pain in Kansas, he thinks,
lifting his horn and watching for the cue,
when they hear about Surf City and believe it.

The Beloved

I wrote this fine glossy poem
about how the true beloved is always ineffable,
the one at the palace window
when the purple light of storm astounds the forest,
the one whose touch is the breeze of April,
the one with breasts of pearl swaying urgent toward the mouth of dream,
cloud-sister of Grace Kelly,
always finally that one in azure kimono

and never the contingent one who flosses
and collides with you in the kitchen
and wants forever to lose five pounds
and notices the smell of your sneakers
and remembers guys with stronger arms.
I wrote the poem and felt kind of brave
and rather ineffable myself
and I kind of saw Apollo in the mirror

so then I published the poem in a smooth journal
dedicated to the Other World that words can make—
world, or only a superb hotel?—

so then my wife reads the poem
and she looks at me: her gray-green eyes
moving in those subtle motions that eyes make
when they're anxious to see something true.

Looking into her eyes then I feel
not like a bad husband really but like a guy
half an inch shorter than he thought
whose poem didn't have the guts to be complicated.

Not Us

He had congestive heart failure with fluid in the lungs
and she had a tumorous kidney removed.
All this last month! But the thing is,
they are not us. That's the whole thing.
They
are not us. Once this concept is grasped, the whole picture becomes
clear and makes good sense. Those four words say it all,
They are not us. It sounds simple yet it means so much.
To begin with, they
are at least twenty-three years older than us—
but that's not the main point, that's actually kind of a distraction
because the central essence of the matter is
THEY ARE NOT US
                          okay and it should just
stay that way stay that way it should
obviously I mean let's keep I mean the lines have to be clear:

they just are not us
which seems a big mistake on their part but really it's not their fault
it's just—

in the hospital that's *them*
and we are simply the ones who send them a soberly attractive card
saying "How awful"
so then we have sent them a card.
We sent a card (because "How awful") so that's done

and there's no reason
to think that card flies up into the night sky
and roars looping beyond sound among invisible clouds
looping in silent fury of speed till some year some day it flies down
soberly attractive and slips quietly how awful under your door my love
and my door.

The Schuylkill

Deep deep in December
driving the icy Schuylkill Expressway at 1:05 A.M.
I might have been really beautiful
as I listened to Dylan sing "He Was a Friend of Mine"
beautiful in how I understood it
but no one (the world) will ever know this—
the Schuylkill just let my beauty atomize like nothing
through the dark shadow-panes of one small black car—

there is something wrong with the whole setup.

A Good Thing

One way it can happen, is Huey Meaux might listen
to a tape from Beaumont while he's cutting hair
in his barber shop in Winnie, and it's T-Baby Green,
all right but in between the T-Baby Green numbers
there's this other voice: this voice that goes
to the heart. So Huey Meaux calls up Big Sambo and says
"Who's this?" and the big guy says "That's Barbara Lynn"
so he brings her from Beaumont over to the barber shop
(she has a slight limp, she's nineteen, she smiles shyly)
and Huey Meaux says she and her mom can meet him at Cosimo's
in New Orleans. And it happens there, and it's
the good thing.
        Another way it can happen might be
it's Bon Ton Garlow who hears her, Barbara Lynn, this voice
and how she plays her guitar left-handed
and he brings her tape to Huey Meaux but Huey's not sure,
but then one night Bon Ton Garlow takes Huey Meaux
to the Ten Acre Club outside Beaumont and there she is
with the voice that goes to the heart. So Huey catches on
and they make the good thing, the record,
and Cosimo Matassa gets it taken by Harry Finfer's label
and so it has happened.
        Or it might happen another way;
there can be a third way, and a fourth—
                there has to be luck—

but at least it can happen;
                        and if it doesn't, well,
then the world will have lost a good thing,
though the world being the world and not a lover
will never notice.

18,000 CDs

Suppose a good photographer in 2022 A.D. takes a picture
of 18,000 compact discs
thrown away in a toppled pile
at a California landfill or a landfill near Memphis
(a few of the titles and artists' names readable or half-readable,
rock, pop, reggae, ska, rap, hiphop, blues—

Mississippi John Hurt;
"Too Much Sugar for a Dime" by Henry Threadgill;
"Start with the Soul" by Alvin somebody;
Lydia Mendoza; "Love Bites like a something";
Anne Finch & the Midnighters; Toots & the Maytals;
"Going Places" by Herb Alpert & the Tijuana Brass . . .)

I would want a copy of that photograph,
I would keep it on my wall
fair creature of an hour
for as long as possible.

Campaign Promise

Under my Administration
(in which each Cabinet member will have many, many long legal pads)

if you were standing frozen in sweated confusion
at the Personal Furnishings rack
in a giant department store five days before Christmas
wearing a woolly jacket that belonged to someone long gone
and trying not to seem dangerous
under silver and scarlet decorations with no conception
of adequate reply to tremendous departures

you'd be a notable American event.

Shnordink's Butterfly

Shnordink? Oh I suppose he has a few good clumpies.
He's not terrible. That one about the moth or butterfly in the graveyard
is pretty good. He has some talent.
Wait a second. Shnordink . . . Say,
is he friends with Audrey Rosedorf
who writes those arrogant reviews in *Muskmelon Quarterly*?
He is? Interesting. Actually,
there's something ultimately hollow in Shnordink,
there's a telltale streak of falsity, a tinniness,
a kind of damp-nosed insidious posing,
a quality of trying-to-play-ball-like-the-bigger-boys . . .
It's as if Rosedorf's absurdly stiff-necked high-handedness had—
What? He did?
Shnordink said I was important?
An important clumper with enviable imaginative flair?
That's interesting. Actually,
I'm pleased to hear it, simply because
Shnordink is not an idiot (whatever his limitations);
I think he has been underestimated in some quarters.
Actually, I'm thinking of reviewing his latest.
A few of those clumpies are, um, rather marvelous, and
the book as a whole, I'm going to say, is quirky and engaging.

In the hillside cemetery accented with circles of petunias and irises,
a creature borne on translucent blue-green wings

rests momentarily atop one stone or another
and then launches itself anew.

Big Picture

At 2 A.M. when I checked on my sleeping four-year-old
she was turned around on her bed with the covers kicked off
and since the house was rather cool I lifted her and turned her
as gently as I could to bring her head back to her pillow
whereupon she, not really waking, opened her eyes and said

"I was going to make a big picture—
but then . . ." And she frowned as if both amused and faintly exasperated
by the impossibility of explaining all the nuances
of what had prevented the making of her big picture;
her eyes closed, and by the time I got the quilt over her
she was gone to the world of sleep.
                              And I realized
the metaphor! I didn't miss it! I saw
                              our lives—
our careers—and I went to my notebook.
This beauty would not slip away. Oh it might have slipped,

I might have let it dissolve into a half-memory
then into nothing but the vague sense any parent has
that one's child has said some fabulous funny deep things.
But instead, I saved it!
                    And I made this, reader.
It will exist always, for me, for you, and for generations yet unborn.
In its way it is a kind of Gibraltar in the history of culture.
Thank heaven I've done it! Now I can rest.

New Thing

It is true there were three *very* big things last year.
Last year was a big year—with those three whopping phenoms,
two of which were solid mahogany with teak accessories
while the third was gray stone with magnesium rivets
and very wide. Thus last year brought much.

But now here is this present thing. What to say?
It is true
this present thing is small, with a narrow edge.
Clearly it will not fly far nor displace tons of mud.

Contrast the four major events of two months ago,
all of which were (though not perhaps gigantic like the phenoms of last year)
arguably, with their sheetrock siding
and their brickwork turrets and their reflector panels
and foldout snap-down digitized display kits, quite big.
Obviously

bigger than this. It is undeniable.

But a cold shake of spring sun has just shone
like a white spray like flung boulder-broken spume
on the high-reefed phone wires between
those tossing green-trope archetypal pines
and here today is this
new thing.

Separated Father

Driving along the city's edge at night
he obeys all traffic signals with chilly prudence.
God might be watching for an excuse to nail him.
He has ceased to live in the house where his daughter lives.
What could be more wrong?
Yet the car is running smoothly; it doesn't know
what kind of man is at the wheel. Indeed
most people seem unable to read on his face
what he has done. Lone cowboy of the night
beyond civilization, he feels ice-gloved
in the unmistakable primacy of self,
who used to think he'd do anything
for his little girl. When he drives past the house
at 2 A.M., slowly, to see her dark window
and believe she is sleeping soundly, he recognizes himself
as protagonist of more than one rather dreary short story
but now it's him,
                    it's him
and the moon is so bright:
above his car and later above his tiny new apartment
it is so damned
bright that no one (not his wife, not any smart or wise person)
can tell him it isn't romantic. Unfortunately

it is romantic. So
he has a new phone, and he has one mint wrapped in silver
from a restaurant called La Famiglia, where no one knew he was a dad;
and he'll phone the woman who changed the meaning of joy.

Divorced Fathers and Pizza Crusts

The connection between divorced fathers and pizza crusts
is understandable. The divorced father does not cook
confidently. He wants his kid to enjoy dinner.
The entire weekend is supposed to be fun. Kids love
pizza. For some reason involving soft warmth and malleability

kids approve of melted cheese on pizza
years before they will tolerate cheese in other situations.
So the divorced father takes the kid and the kid's friend
out for pizza. The kids eat much faster than the dad.
Before the dad has finished his second slice,

the kids are playing a video game or being Ace Ventura
or blowing spitballs through straws, making this hail
that can't quite be cleaned up. There are four slices left
and the divorced father doesn't want them wasted,
there has been enough waste already; he sits there

in his windbreaker finishing the pizza. It's good
except the crust is actually not so great—
after the second slice the crust is basically a chore—
so you leave it. You move on to the next loaded slice.
Finally there you are amid rims of crust.

All this is understandable. There's no dark conspiracy.
Meanwhile the kids are having a pretty good time

which is the whole point. So the entire evening makes
clear sense. Now the divorced father gathers
the sauce-stained napkins for the trash and dumps them

and dumps the rims of crust which are not
corpses on a battlefield. Understandability
fills the pizza shop so thoroughly there's no room
for anything else. Now he's at the door summoning the kids
and they follow, of course they do, he's a dad.

Heavy Trash

What is that man doing?
He is clumping through the snow toward the municipal trash barrel
next to General Wayne Park.

What is in the black trash bag he is carrying?
It looks so heavy!
It is amazingly heavy. It contains
two Philadelphia phonebooks and a Children's Health Encyclopedia
and three drawing pads and an illustrated history of baseball.

That's all? That doesn't sound so heavy.
But they are full of ice—that is, they have become
blocks of pulp stiff with frozen rain.

Explain.
I will explain, I want to explain.
He is a divorced father.

And?
And divorced fathers cannot evade absurdities.

Is that an explanation?
There was an apartment . . . Then the trunk of an old car . . .

What is he doing now?
He is pounding the trash bag with a stone from a stone wall
to make it fit down into the trash barrel.

Should he be arrested?
No. The police have less absurd things to focus on.

Is there meaning in this?
It's about how some endings never end.

The Fedge

All the fedge and the drammel, the fedge
and all the drammel—there is
all this up the middle this fedge
and this drammel, such that I wizen,
I wizen and waf-waf unflashly,
unflashly and unlike a diamond
with the main thing away—
the main thing the What For thing over *there*—
over *there*—

away what I did fathom and enter into wholly
what I might now fathom and wholly enter into:
out all at the corners, past a bleached fence,
around the crumbly grecktic brick-silence wall—

there was more of me to be and is
if I am he who said on a bench in Waltham one deep true thing
of Emily Dickinson or Gregoire Turgeon
and if I am he whose son stood
happy, central, conversant
in Orlando Magic peejays with his hand on my shoulder

but I do not keep that here or do not stay there—

instead the slog and shog of the drammel pervades
and the fedge my head amid—
for numerous sensible reasons this occurs
for countable reasons no doubt
                              but this is to say
I am *not unaware*

that all this manage of drammel and fedge,
so much copage with through the middle that mudge
and down the frown the various fraddel
is overloadedly multiplexly only shoof shuff,
mere waf-waf near drained of What truly For.

Parkersburg

I will arise now and put on a black baseball cap and go
to Parkersburg. It will fit me,
the cap will, and it will be black,
the sneakers on my feet will be purple,
and I will not have shaved for three days.
The day will be rainy and cool
and I will wear an old jacket of pale wool
that was once my Uncle Lew's.
And go to Parkersburg.

On a bus I may go
or in an old car full of tapes—
Elmore James; Fred McDowell; Taj Mahal; the Kinks.
Into the town of Parkersburg
on a day so rainy and cool. And I will be
terrifically untroubled if anyone thinks I am strange,
in fact everything about this day will be a ratification
of how I am not them; and my manner, though courteous,
will tend to make them suspect that they are boring.
They will wonder why they have no purple sneakers. Cool

and lightly rainy in Parkersburg
and me all day there exactly as if my belief
had long been firm; not forgetting for one minute
how I felt years ago listening to "I'm Different" by Randy Newman

and the sacred tears in my eyes at that time.
I and my black baseball cap will enter a tavern

and there we will read a French poet with such concentration
it will be like I *am* that guy. Then pretty soon
in another tavern it is a Spanish poet whom I read
with similar effect. In Parkersburg!
Oh my Parkersburg . . . And I swear,
though I might not meet a lonely marvelous slim woman with black hair
it will still be as if I did.

The Issue Here

Not the semen of some dippy smug plump guy
with hairs growing out of his pimples
and chatter about pro wrestling and Metallica
or ways to minimize income tax,
not *his* semen, that's *not*
what I'm talking about!
Christ, that's not even RELEVANT.
I'm
talking about beautiful glistening
Romantic semen of witty passion
adorably summoned in a surprising classy hotel
that has character!
Delia, Donna, Diana, Dolores,
don't you hear me? *That's*
what I'm talking about.

Seven Baskets

And then I sprang from the silver taxi
onto the vermilion carpet in front of a certain fine hotel,
a hotel tall and confident with windows buttressed in gold
like the aura that buttressed my casually athletic gestures
though this was in fact the hotel where in a previous life
I suffered a certain humiliation amid a committee
and/or when a woman embarrassed for me shook her head
and changed the subject—but now that past was to be
redeemed with such comic fullness I had to chuckle
striding through the great glass doors and nodding
very slightly to young dressy people who recognized me
and murmured behind magazines about my importance.
I was now a necessary part of something very large
without which humanity would seem a petty mechanical thing
and I flowed along the lobby on the steady wave
of being indispensable. Then from an elevator stepped

Deirdre who had seemed to ignore me last year
but now with a new blonde streak in her hair
rather obviously indicating her need for approval
she saw me suddenly and stopped and her cheeks went pink
and I knew, I knew I had only to propose a drink
and in less than two hours, in just seventy-five minutes
we'd be in the huge bed of my room Room 507
with Deirdre making little sounds of almost desperate hunger.
And this was all clear of any moral clouding

because I was not now married despite what was true
in my other life, that life all stuffed and bricked
with memories and the shrinkage induced by recriminations.
So then for hours at least five hours the eager breasts of Deirdre
served as a cinematic focus around which
the zest of my being constellated itself while
everything I did was music, my every motion sang itself
like the Dell-Vikings when they sang "Whispering Bells"
and Deirdre was lit up like a peach entering God's mouth
because she knew she could never get luckier than this!
I felt sweetly sorry for her amid the cascading pleasure
because I sensed that in the morning she would neatly vanish
into some gray traffic of transmission trouble and fiancé
while I washed my hair and then in the gold-appointed café

I drank the hotel's superb coffee and said "Mallarmé"
at precisely the moment needful to silence several critics
who in the other life might smother my head in Handi-Wrap phrases
but not now! And then roaming humorously with bright teeth
and knowledge of Deirdre still on my lips I arrived at a gleaming gym
for an intense three-on-three game which I caused my team to win
despite the lunges of heavier men whose procedures are logical
by making seven baskets in a row just when the action was hottest.
Seven! Including two hook shots and a reverse layup. Yes.
And then by a process tedious to explain in words
yet strangely lubricated and offhand
the basketball victory led to a party in someone's mansion

where both rangy Teresa and confectionary Connie
used dancing as a way to compete for my attention.
On the breezy moonlit balcony I knew sublimity was available
in several forms including astoundingly witty conversation
but sex was the most convenient—I could take it or leave it

without a shadow of anxiety but why not take it
as Teresa and Connie both seemed hypnotized by my flexing shoulders
and my candid gaze which set a new standard for self-assurance
in the history of athletic Dell-Viking poets.
With hilariously swift panache between rooms upstairs
I gave thrills almost frighteningly sheer to Teresa and Connie in turn,
not failing to reap full unambivalent recompense, and then
I strolled back to the moonlit balcony and wrote
a poem so rich it made normal living look like sawdust
and then I published it in ten prestigious journals
and just acted gently modest when people said it was great.

Seven Boxes

Seven boxes, all rather heavy; seven boxes filled with paper;
cardboard boxes purchased many years ago from U-Haul;
they are not huge, but truly quite heavy; a strong man
would not want to lift two of them at once.

Seven boxes and they squeak very faintly as they jostle
in the back of a neighbor's pickup truck, or maybe
in the trunk and on the back seat of my daughter's car.
It's quite a load! Something had to be done. Perspective

changes. It's a cloudy day and hotter than you'd want
but the upstairs room had to be cleared out, the time
had come and the day had come and people already chose
a few keepsakes and so now the seven boxes ride trembly

to the dump and I must describe this—must DESCRIBE
this very sharply, incisively, describe it VERY vividly:

So the small truck or long car in 2041 takes the turn
onto the unpaved curving road to where you can legally dump
(somehow the idea of recycling all that paper has not arisen
today, the recycling option is somehow not there today) and

now the strong hands of perhaps my son's best friend's son
or my niece Georgia's husband reach firmly and lift
the first box and the next and the next and heave them,
heave all seven boxes onto the great pile or down into

the great trough: all seven boxes. Because the day is,
you know, a day for getting things done, and then later,
three hours later, in 2041, there'll be a barbecue.
That's a good thing. In the car or truck someone says

something humorously respectful
about how much a person can write
and nukketa nukketa nukketa the tires go
rolling down the curvy road.

Schnetzer Day

This amazing fine song comes on the radio
the day after my death,
it's Greenie Schnetzer and the Generous Glands
singing "Defrocked Bishop of Love" and it is gorgeous.
The song combines the feel of "Get a Job" by the Silhouettes
with the sexy speed of "Roadrunner" as performed by
Joan Jett and the Blackhearts, and someone hears it
and realizes all this. Less than a day has passed
since my demise, and someone feeling comfortable
in a soft pair of old jeans suddenly remembers
the calm weary face of his mother, or sister,
a few weeks before she died of cancer, and also
sees back to his father one sad Christmas
saying "This Bulgarian wine is surprisingly good"
and has a sense of how people keep trying. Also
someone wearing an old herringbone jacket in a hallway
sings "Gypsy gal" softly and it means a great deal.
And around a corner comes a certain potential romantic partner
and says "Lunch?"
                        Meanwhile I'm dead.
In a school gym some guy makes an absurd hook shot
from downtown, nothing but net, with a certain Susan watching.
And a person wearing a Portland Sea Dogs cap
finishes a poem by rhyming "tyro" with "Cairo"
and places warm forehead against a cool pane of glass.
And there's more, involving children's games and tragic visions,

but already it seems obvious that my death is a bad mistake—
just think of Greenie Schnetzer!—
and I guess in fact I'd better live forever.

You and Yours

Your view yours of over there of your outlook of from where you stand
is all discolored—all pasted and pocked, mucked,
all incommodious and unaccommodatable—ulterior of orbit—
your view yours—it is all striated with streaks of
overthereness. So it's no wonder—

I mean your thing of "your thing" has such stucco of perverse youhood
with your Symbio-Ziggurat Semiconductor Squab Tractate Corp. of Tennessee
and smoking a Lucky Strike wearing a UNLV cap
dashing down into the subway for the Farid al-Din local
and of someone's Uncle Henry on the Expressionist phase of Schoenberg
and of Charlene in her burnt-orange shorts
dangling down her brown toes from the cottonwood branch
into the Mylamoseby with its weedy clotting muck.
You you . . .

So it's no wonder you heedlessly glance away toward
a professor of astronomy or a sandwich called Hazel's Second Heaven
when I sing "under that apple sucklin' tree, oh yeah"

no wonder since crudely and stiffly and chunk-plunkly you have
Morocco and morocco-damask and morocco-leather
and a *krupka* of chamomile moiré
and Art Tatum doing "Basil Folie" at Jibby's Chicken Shack,
paper lanterns of Noguchi and the sad watertower of Quanteeko,
Svetlana from Rostov fixing an old popcorn machine

and what occurred with a butcher's daughter from Luxembourg
yeah you have your Zachary J. under a plum tree
recalling the House of Always Cous Cous
and your Béchamel of red-legged partridges
and your sturgeon's head drenched in champagne . . .

You have also your pain—you know which—that pain—
that one in the steel net of memory
chugging on those half-lit elliptic tracks
through stations where I hold no ticket—
in view of those deep defiles and files, of your notion
of what happened with you in the tenebrous room of love betrayed
where Mademoiselle Vatnaz was at the piano

it's only natural that you DON'T GET IT when I say
"Gabriella in the tall grass" or "Eric on the last stair"—

you *think* you get it—because you can frame up
a category and you can poke my oddments into the category
oh *thanks* a *ton!* To dissolve into a category,
is that why I marched this far across stony hills and airports
lugging these bags and parcels bedecked with surprising stickers?

Dennis Pravy Speaks

People say to me they ask me how did I do so much stuff,
how did I design two separate Internet crossroads convention clubs
within the past two years along with over a dozen
electro-self-scan sites for the use of my techniques of
self-multiplication via Growth-Via-Stress, along with
the photo-cartoon guidepaks that accompany each site
with blink-activated digital GZL-LR personality-coded tour modules
okay, like how did I *do* all that while also never quitting
the triathlon/hammer-throw in which I've qualified
for regional pro trials in my weight class six years running
and also you know playing bass for Hypertropic Bratwurst
and authoring and self-laptop-deskless-simulcast-publishing
the Dennis Pravy Stopless Brain Futurecream series of
dream-crime adventures with user-option victory-extension plots,
seven volumes published so far and the last three picked up
by Scum Warrior Programz for like national distribution
and my eighth volume due next month,
actually like practically the same day as
Hypertropic Bratwurst's third album "Why Snuff the Rooster"—

—Dennis, people say, Dennis,
how in the hell do you *do* all that?
And what I say is
Oh man, man, HOW COULD I NOT?
I mean look at this world, like, have you *noticed*?
This fucking world man it's like a watermelon

just begging to drip all down your sugar-sucking face!
It's like this beautiful woman like what's-her-face
the one who was on "Twin Peaks" only she has five breasts!
Five, man, and your job is just to keep them all happy!
This fucking world! It's like "Sleep? Who sleeps?"
The world is like this huge eighteen-wheeler loaded with rocks
and it's coming down this long hill right behind you going BRAAHHMMP
but it's also, at the same time, it's also this Hollywood dessert item
with five pineapples jogging just ahead of you on this beach in Baja
going like "Do you have a blanket I could share?"
It's all that, man. The world says "Do me now,
you can sleep when you're dead."
And I'm sure we will.
Okay, so that's your interview, right?
Mention the album twice, at least—it gives people a focus—
it's like "Fuck! What do I do about Dennis Pravy?"
and the answer is Buy the album!
But the real answer—the real answer is like UNKNOWN.
I mean, if I knew the real answer, man,
you think I'd be here with you?

Sourdough

If abruptly it appears that we're all just sandwiches
transformed by chewing, all just appetitive organisms
walking our little walks toward auspicious mating,
writing our plotty little novels about
progress toward mating, discussing some shoddy glittered
movie about little bumps on the path toward
auspicious mating, all eating our thick sandwiches
on sourdough bread and floating toward cancer
not now but ten years later or thirty-five years later
on the ticking schedule for well-shod well-shirted
healthy blah—
temporary skin coating temporary flesh
all saying "a positive outlook" and
"reassess the priorities" amid the layers of sandwich—

the generality is what pulls toward Void.
Quickly identify the particular restaurant,
the partic. street, a partic. funny scene
in that shoddy movie, drink a Lynchburg Lemonade
and quote something from page 77 of a partic. book
and say I love that, actually.

But when the faves, the gems, the trinkets of perception
flip one day from one-by-one lovability to repellent microscopic triviality
what to do then? Invent a religion maybe, or move
a thousand cinderblocks by hand across a yard?

Landscape #11

Mr. Gleeders trims the shrubs alongside New Life Foursquare Church.
Dokie passes by in his Cherokee.
In the concrete bench area between Pay Less Shoes and the courthouse
a gangly girl scuffs the heels of her sandals.
What's her name? She's looking down. Cigarette butts. She wants
to feel better.

Small trees flicker modestly in the long-day hot breeze.
Well, it's not as if . . .

Sandra tells her son Jason she'll be home by seven
to drive him to the Scouts cookout. She just has to finish these invoices.

No one is visiting the Heavenly Bride Catholic Cemetery
on Flinderation Road. In the peeling white house
up the next hill, a baby coughs and goes back to sleep.

invoices
diehard
peeling

On the loading platform at the Bud Light distributor
five young women smoke. They see Dokie pass by,
they meet his look. "That's right, we've got it
and we know it won't last forever."

Edgar Lee Masters and Sherwood Anderson sit quiet
at a table in heaven. Bare wood table, nothing on it.

The sign outside Kentucky Fried Chicken suggests
we can Defeat the Dark Side with a bucket of fried.
Dokie doesn't smile as he passes in his Cherokee
but he thinks about it.

Small trees flicker. Hot breeze.
Behind the community college a shirtless guy shoots a basketball—
it rattles in—but the net is so frayed . . .

He gets his young thick wife to shoot, it's an air ball way way short,
it bounces down a paved incline, he fetches it.
She thinks of watering the tomatoes at home. Try to be happy.

and we know it won't last forever

Jason checks his acne in the mirror
"Yeah fuck you" he tells the mirror, practicing.

It's not as if—

Tomorrow night is championship wrestling on TV, with Grandma.

Small trees flicker
Heavenly Bride
the net so frayed
hot long breeze
                    This is me being bard of America
baby coughs and goes back to sleep

Dokie pitches tonight for the Moxahala Badgers.
The Badgers are 2 and 8.
Some diehard fans'll be there.

'89 Ford Fiesta "runs good" $750 call B. J. Norris

That's right, we've got it

Flinderation Road

Small trees flicker modestly in the long hot-day breeze—
it's not as if they could run away.

Nebraska Novel

Chapter One.
While Coby put his denim jacket on, Lanna rolled her coveralls
and handed them to Wyatt, who put them on the seat of the tractor.
Then the thub skelled and the frobbies wackled up shorfing
over the brown water. Coby glanced his hat and wiped his belt
and folded his brows and blew his cuffs. "Yeah, Coby," said Lanna,
with a smishing of her dark dables.
Wyatt hopped into the tractor, beside her coveralls and the janker.
He handed the janker to Coby who handed it to Lanna.
Then she placed her hand on his hand on the janker.
Wyatt watched from the corner of his crinkle.
And the wind cheffed over the brown water.

Chapter Two.
Coby woke with his denims grunked on the cold wood floor
and his arm polgoed over Lanna's bresh. Outside, Wyatt whistled
while he poured oil into the tractor. "Shap dolly day,
grass on the dray, will you put the puddin' on, wish I may"
was what Wyatt sang in the creeling light of the molehumped yard.
Lanna woke and said "Yeah, you, Coby"
and the frobbies began their droomatious shorfing again.

Chapter Three.
The tractor fregged a little and medged a good bit
but soon Wyatt was jouncing along the road
past the long reaches of brown water. The road was dirt

and dirt the road and this was all like it was. It was
like so. Then Wyatt stretched for Coby and yanked him up
to the tractor seat and Lanna came flammering
and hoikled right up beside them. Coby took off his denim jacket
in the crispy sunshine and he handed it to Wyatt.
Wyatt handed it back. Lanna took it and rolled it up
inside her coveralls. It made a lump and Coby's stump made a thump
as they passed over a hump near the brown pump
while Lanna's dables kept on smishing darkly.

Chapter Four.
Oh the land was big, and wet and dry. The land is huge and a whopper the sky
and the smibnibs are eternal. Big was the land
and they knew it in the pulchy cribs of their orgs,
as the thub skelled, with a crimshinsky noise,
and the wind cheffed briskly over the brown water.

Bookstore Dazzle

In this compelling and beguiling novel, a young man
finds himself shanghaied into a tailspin vortex
of deceit and desire where nothing is what it seems
and insidious schemes multiply beneath bright pants
and hypnotic expensive dresses. Harvey enters a world
where every kiss is a lie and every lie is a wish
and every turn brings a new confetti of adjectives.
It is a ride into the deepest organs of America.
A child has vanished, a detective has made a pledge,
a dancer at the Fox Leap Swan Dive has changed her name.
Three generations of women face three rites of passage
as they struggle to define a woman's dignity
against the destructive magnetism of a family curse
in a gossamer web of memory, money, betrayal and lust.
Seldom have the confused hungers of the Seventies
been so darkly tied to the gross appetites of the Eighties.
Into this witches' brew tumbles a homeless guitarist
named Gazpacho driving a stolen Land Rover,
chewing ginseng, and hoping to buy forest land with sex.
But a strange figure calling himself Radio Death interferes,
with bloody results, and the midget twins Melg and Felg
collide with destiny during the Mummers Parade
as Darla learns more than she ever dreamed
about her mother's past in Copenhagen and Bangkok.
Darla will never be the same and neither will the reader
as the pages fly by like days in a world strangely coherent

and supremely nonsleepy, until the night when Harvey finds
a certain necklace on a certain neck and a thick book
like a strong hand that shows him what it is to be a man
not petty not petty not petty in a time of hypodermic fear
and oily hips and sudden steel and what we are and what it is
to know the crimson rose of infinite yearning hugely blooms
against a black velvet field, hugely and nothing else.

The Opaque

We crave it because we feel it is secretly us
after the ideas wearing name tags have had their big convention.
But that's an idea; that's not it.

Bumpy muddy fields with stands of scruffy trees.

Blueprints for the wiring of public buildings in Singapore.

The life lived in a purple Volkswagen
parked next to the Almstead Tree Company in New Rochelle.

A quick-stepping woman in a corridor, moving away;
her calves.

In the opaque, there are only examples.

Venezuela.

Any one word said over and over. Opaque.

Ed Skoog. Opaque. Mitch Green. Opaque.
Serina Mammon. Out of reach.

Gusto of deer hunters. Venison draining.

Speckly smudged static of when we are too tired, when are we too tired
for one more example?

Seventy-year-old twins who sing together of baby Jesus.

Juliette Gréco singing at Le Boeuf sur le Toit
and how some guy named Bernard interpreted her phrasing.
Years back, years back years back.

Hundreds of people standing in rain to watch golf.

The next thing, the next thing you get stuck on
before it becomes a handy metaphor . . .

A news item in Arabic about stolen bicycles.

If there were a tribe of Indians called the Opakis,
their way of stitching beaver pelts would be opaque.

Those gray people politely serving around the edges of your life
and how they can stand it.

Bumpy muddy fields with stands of scruffy trees
and why the trees bother to stand up.

Silence of a stuffed bag of laundry.
Laundry, laundry.

That blonde woman on the subway, she wasn't Sophie
she couldn't have been Sophie

Cheddar cheese soup

The waitress who served me my cheddar cheese soup today
without a word and walked out of the restaurant
ten minutes later in her gray blue winter jacket

The pain of that person you said you loved six years ago.

We get tired, but what would it mean to be tired enough?

Congested heart of a man not yet a character in a novel
committing murder this very hour in Tennessee.

What peels away from or pokes out through yesterday's
poem, poamb, poeem, pom-pom
in that black behind black ink . . .

Tintex—Japalac—
Kish & Sons Electric. Zelda's Diner.
Combo Basket at the Big Top.

Mister Thasildar of Bombay ignoring three young dying prostitutes
in a parlor of his Naazma bordello.

Beans in the middle of the night.

Who built this tunnel? How long is this tunnel?
Does it go somewhere? Oh never mind,
here comes the light of day.

Route 302

Six years old, my son is dangerously smaller than the world;
at dusk on Route 302
suddenly I feel the disparity
while he sleeps beside me in the front seat.
Extensiveness without care—

beside Route 302 there is
that long slanted yard, the green strangely
darkened already now after sunset, in the shadow
of a hill; at the top of the yard, a white house
with no lights; empty; and behind this house
a further yard, and a shed; dried earth
on the tools in that shed . . .
Past the shed there is a rocky field
rising to a ridge; over this ridge there is
a wider field of beans (bitter and hard, those beans,
with no interest in bitterness or hardness) and then a strip of woods
already quite dark. Those woods—
and my boy here.
                    And what else? Through that strip of woods
there is a trail leading downhill to a clearing—I know
there have surely been funny laughing boys
ranging down that trail but not now after dusk
not in the world of night coming beyond
Route 302. Downhill to a clearing where
two red houses stand quiet completely;

the red paint now is so dark; one light burns
over the back porch of the taller house but
not with power to undarken even the nearest trees.
The dirt driveway curves around into a field
in which several old sedans and two pickups are rusting
with no tires. And what?
The driveway reaches an unpaved road. Beyond this road
the forest (—*my boy sleeping here*—) the forest stands thick:
density of tangle of dark limbs; and
half a mile straight back through complete darkness
(if someone could go) amid the crowding trees
there is a creek that flows almost silently not seen
over granite chunks that lie randomly along the creekbed; and
across the creek in darkness there is more forest
too thick for walking, too densely tangled
with no interest in being densely tangled
out there, all out there *extending*
beside Route 302
after sunset
and my boy thus not safe!

All this
too apparent for half a minute on Route 302
until we pass through a village and I can
gear down and be like a normal sensible driver
who stays on the road.

Why Must We Write?

Because of the wave. And because
the streets radiate into three more neighborhoods
than we have even ever heard of, in our own town!
Because everything just left. And because
those people at the table laughed
when we didn't know about tequila or Nietzsche.
Then came the dead streetlamp.
Hence we must write. Also because

for 3 percent of us there will be fabulous jobs
in which mainly we can just read books for thirty years
and talk about the ones we've read and the ones we haven't read.
Also for another 14 percent of us there will be
decent tolerable jobs permitting in rather brownish ways
a tolerable amount of the fine wordy dreaming
we will die saying we need more of.
If we write, if we write a great deal, if we stay home from the video store
and write more
then we really might get into the 14 percent and even into the lucky 3 percent
and even, who knows, even into the magical .3 percent
whose names we all try to remember—
to remember because otherwise there is only the wave of forgetting
which is so common, so K-Mart,
so have-another-basket-of-ribs-and-die. So thus

we write. Because of the wave;
because the castle is of sand. And because
the pressure is immense of taxis and taxes and toxic waste
and Internet pathways to maximizing investment growth
and low-fat trimline high-gloss budget-conscious workout plans
and the thing that surpasses your current audio system

and because Patricia turned away as if bored.
In the room where people were getting their coats, pleased with their coats
and mentioning favorite sectors of northern Italy,
Patricia turned away from me as if I was boring to her.
Wait till she sees my books! But also because

that ten-year-old boy uncombed and scuffing
at sunset on the Amtrak platform in Bridgeport
looked strangely familiar and seemed to matter
terribly somehow and we did not speak to him.

The Missing Poem

It would have been dark but not lugubrious. It would have been
fairly short but not slight. It would have contained a child
saying something inadvertently funny that was not said by my daughter,
something strangely like what your daughter or sister said once
if you could remember. The child's voice flies across
a small parking lot where, in one of the cars,
a man and a woman sit listening to the silence between them.
The child's voice probably hurts them momentarily
with a sense of beauty apparently very possible
yet somehow out of reach. In the missing poem this is
implied, conveyed, transmitted without being flatly said.
And it does a dissolve into the look of a soccer field
after a game—the last three or four players walk
slowly away, their shin-guards muddy, their cleats caked,
one player dragging a net bag full of soccer balls—
the players seem to have known what it was all for
yet now they look somehow depleted and aimless there
at the field's far end; and a block away on a wood-grainy porch
the eyes of a thin woman sixty-three years old search the shadows
in each passing car, as the poem recalls what she wants to recall.
Hours later the field is dark

and the hills are dark and later even Firehouse Pizza has closed.
In the missing poem all this pools into a sense of how much
we must cherish life; the world will not do it for us.
This idea, though, in the missing poem is not smarmy.

Remember when you got the news of the accident—
or the illness—in the life of someone
more laced into your life than you might have thought;
the cool flash of what serious is. Well,
the missing poem brings that. Meanwhile not seeming like
an imitation of Mark Strand or Mark Doty or Mark Jarman!
Yet not like just another Halliday thing either.
Instead it would feel like a new dimension of the world,
the real world we imagine. With lightness!
With weight *and* lightness and, on the hypothetical radio,
that certain song you almost forgot to love.